Pre-Historic Man
by Manning Ferguson Force

Copyright © 2019 by HardPress

Address:
HardPress
8345 NW 66TH ST #2561
MIAMI FL 33166-2626
USA
Email: info@hardpress.net

GN
766
F6
LOCKED
CASE

THE LIBRARY
OF
THE UNIVERSITY
OF CALIFORNIA

PRESENTED BY
PROF. CHARLES A. KOFOID AND
MRS. PRUDENCE W. KOFOID

Pre-Historic Man.

DARWINISM AND DEITY.

The Mound Builders.

By M. F. FORCE.

CINCINNATI:
ROBERT CLARKE & CO.
1873.

The Bancroft Library

Bancroft Library
University of California
WITHDRAWN

Pre-Historic Man.

DARWINISM AND DEITY.

THE MOUND BUILDERS.

By M. F. FORCE.

CINCINNATI:
ROBERT CLARKE & CO.
1873.

These Papers were read before the

CINCINNATI LITERARY CLUB:

PRIMITIVE MAN—March 21, 1868;

DARWINISM AND DEITY—January 13, 1872;

THE MOUND BUILDERS—April 15, 1873.

THE

PRIMITIVE INHABITANTS

OF

WESTERN EUROPE.

In 1829, an excavation made in the shore of the Lake of Zurich, near Meilen, brought up fragments of wooden piles and other remains, which attracted no attention at the time, and were thrown, with the mud in which they were imbedded, into the deep part of the lake.

In the winter of 1853–4, the water in the Swiss lakes fell one foot lower than the mark of 1674, which had been considered the lowest known in history. Several gentlemen of Meilen took advantage of this low water to extend their land into the lake, inclosing portions laid bare, and filling up the inclosed spaces with neighboring mud. · The workmen, as soon as they began to excavate, found the mud, forming the bottom of this portion of the lake, filled with wooden piles, horns and bones of animals, implements of stone, and fragments of pottery. The interest of antiquarians was at once excited. Investigations were set on foot. It was soon found that the shores of the Swiss lakes were

The Primitive Inhabitants

dotted with abounding remains of an ancient people, whose habitations were built in the water, and who passed away without leaving a tradition. Further research found similar remains in Germany and the lakes of Northern Italy. The traces of one such settlement were found adjoining Pliny's villa. Yet Pliny seems to have had no suspicion of their existence—to have heard no tradition of its builders.

The few years that have passed since the discovery of the winter of 1853—4, have been so busily used in the study of these remains, that a new chapter of history has been sketched, the lake dwellers have become a familiar name, and their epoch has become an established starting point for reaching still further back into the past.

Their villages were built in shoal water, in a few cases within twenty feet—sometimes several hundred yards—from the shore. Piles, sometimes whole trunks, sometimes split, were driven within a few feet of each other, and cut off at top so as to make a level surface. In many cases they were filled in between, with stones, for firmness. A boat has been found lying on the bottom, still holding its load of stones, just where it capsized some thousands of years ago. In other cases, the piles were strengthened with cross-pieces. On the outer edge, toward the lake, a wattling of wicker-work prevented waves from washing in.

Over the surface was laid a floor of cross-timbers and saplings ; and this being covered with clay and pebbles, made the groundwork of the settlement. Huts were built in rows. All the huts appear to have been square, and their main timbers to be long piles projecting above

Of *Western Europe.*

the general surface. A weather-boarding of a single plank surrounded each hut at the bottom, keeping out wet. So far no indications have been found of more than a single row of boards being so used. Apparently, each hut contained but one room ; each contained one fire-place of stone slabs. Some had trunks of trees with branches lopped short, as if used for hanging up articles to keep them from the floor. Nearly all had clay weights used in weaving. The sides of the huts were made by weaving small wythes among the upright supports and covering the walls so made with a thick coating of clay. Where the villages were burnt, large fragments are found of the clay with the impression of the burnt wicker-work on the inner side.

The inhabitants kept their domestic animals out in these villages. The researches have already brought up whole museums full of implements of stone, bone, bronze, and iron ; arrow-heads, lance-heads, swords, hatchets, hammers, chisels, knives, needles, pins, hair-pins, brooches, necklaces, and other ornaments ; pottery, linen stuffs, and wearing apparel, and even charred fragments of bread, and seeds of berries and fruits.

We do not yet know certainly the race, language, government, or religion of these people. The pile villages only indicate a certain stage—an early one—of development. Hippocrates mentions villages of this sort in the river Phasis, in Colchis. Herodotus relates that the inhabitants of a similar village in Lake Prasias, in Thrace, escaped unharmed during the invasion of Xerxes. Abulfeda described one such in the Apamean lake, in Syria, in the thirteenth century. The crannogs of Ireland—analogous structures, though used

8 *The Primitive Inhabitants*

only as strongholds to withdraw to in times of danger—continued in use to a later day. A village precisely similar, inhabited by the Indians on the northern coast of South America, was discovered by Ojeda, before 1500, and named by him Venezuela. It is mentioned in Navarrete's account of the voyage, and described more fully in the letters ascribed to Vespucius. The natives of New Guinea, when discovered, dwelt in villages precisely like those of the Swiss lakes. These habitations, therefore, have no ethnological value, but are resorted to by nations in early and rude states, in lake countries, just as steep hills and battlemented castles are resorted to in other ages and situations.

But these people, though rude, were not entirely barbarous. If they navigated the lakes in canoes, each scooped from a single trunk, they fished with hooks that might be used now, and with nets. Their attention to agriculture is indicated by the manure which seemed to have been heaped up and saved, and by their sickles. Though they depended, particularly in the most ancient settlements, largely upon hunting as well as fishing, yet they kept domestic animals—cattle, sheep, goats, and pigs. Their mechanical skill ranged from rudely chipping stone implements to casting and working bronze and iron with some skill. Their pottery, though made by the hand, not with the lathe, and baked in open fires, was sometimes wrought in shapes not without elegance, and ornamented with taste. Fragments of linen cloth have been found, some of which must have been made upon a simple species of loom, and one, embroidered with regular designs in needle-work.

Of Western Europe.

They had some communication with other nations. They had quartz from Gaul; some bits of amber, which must have come from the Baltic; and nephrite, from Asia. A small bar of pure tin has been found, and some vases have thin strips of tin pressed into the surface for ornament. This, with the glass beads found at some of the older settlements, must have been brought to their maritime neighbors by the Phœnicians. It was taken for granted, at first, that their bronze came from the same source; but crucibles have been found with dross yet adhering to the edge; and a well-constructed bronze mold has been discovered. Besides, it has been noticed that the bronze implements which appear most ancient, are modeled after the stone implements that were in use before the introduction of metal; while those made when metal became more common, appear to have been gradually fashioned in shapes better suited to metal. Finally, chemical analysis, by Professor Von Fellenberg, of Berne, has shown that much of the bronze used contains nickel, which is not the case with bronze found elsewhere. Now, in Switzerland, in the vale of Anniviers, mines of copper and nickel are found close together. Hence these early people seem to have been, to some extent, miners.

The remains of food indicate that the villages were inhabited throughout the year. Seeds of fruits and berries mark all the months of summer; beech-nuts and hazel-nuts point to autumn; and the bones of the swan, which visits the Swiss lakes only in December and January, mark the winter. The stores of grain found in one village destroyed by fire, show they laid up food; and the quantity of loose flax and thread indicate that

The Primitive Inhabitants

they had occupation for the indoor season. They found leisure to fabricate ornaments, as well as implements for use. Bracelets, necklaces, brooches, are not rare, and the abundance of hair-pins, ornamented as well as plain, suggests that the ladies of the lakes had ample tresses, and took pride in them. The identity of the grain cultivated, and the weed of southern origin mingled with it, indicate intercourse with southern Europe.

The duration of these settlements must have covered a considerable lapse of time. The amount of remains and refuse could only accumulate in centuries. The settlement of Robenhausen presents proof of a different sort. Here are found the ruins of three settlements, one above the other; the first two apparently destroyed by fire, the last abandoned. The growth of several feet of peat, upon each bed of debris, between it and the next succeeding, shows that a long interval elapsed between the destruction of the successive villages. Moreover, the villages belong to three different stages of civilization—the ages of stone, of bronze, and of iron.

In all parts of the world stone implements appear to have been used first. Then the soft metals, copper and tin, were brought into use. And, finally, when the less obvious iron was detected in its ore, and contrivance for blast heat to smelt it was invented, civilization took another advance. These three stages are represented in the lake dwellings. It is possible, indeed, that three different types of civilization might exist side by side, even in the narrow compass of Switzerland. But they appear, in fact, to have been successive. In the villages where metal is not found, the bones of wild animals predominate; while those belonging to the

Of Western Europe.

bronze epoch abound chiefly with bones of domestic animals. In the first, fox bones are common. In the others, they are few; and skeletons of a large variety of dog appear. Now these different successive stages of society,—though not the pure result of spontaneous effort and development of these people, but stimulated and hastened by intercourse with more advanced nations, —must still represent a period of long duration.

How long this duration was, can not, of course, be determined; but suggestions, which are something more than guesses, have been made. The absence of cat, mouse, or rat, and still more, the entire absence of the domestic fowl, which was introduced into Greece in the time of Pericles, and is first known in Italy by coins struck about a hundred years before Christ, and the presence of the sweet cherry, which was introduced into Italy from the East by Lucullus, fix one limit. These settlements did not last after about the beginning of the Christian era. On the other hand, the remains of birds found are precisely such as are found in Switzerland now. The wild plants and trees of their day are identical, in the minutest particular, with the flora of the same localities at the present day. The bones of only two animals are found that do not live in Switzerland now: the urus, or great ox; and the aurochs, or bison. Cæsar saw both of these in Germany, where, indeed, they did not wholly perish till the middle ages; and although the urus is now extinct, the bison is still preserved in a forest in Lithuania, for the special hunting sports of the Czars. Hence, whatever date may be assigned to the origin of these settlements, it must be within the present geological epoch.

Professor Morlot, of Switzerland, has tried to fix the date from geological data. He noticed in a railroad cut through a bank thrown up, sand and gravel deposit at the mouth of a little stream emptying into one of the lakes, in which, at different depths, were a stratum of rubbish, containing Roman remains, another containing bronze implements, and a third, containing stone implements. In another lake, where, at the mouth of a similar stream, made land has extended into the lake, the remains of a convent, and of one of the lake settlements, denote the position of the shore at the respective dates of these two settlements. M. Morlot argues from the date of the Roman remains in the one case, and of the convent in the other, that the Swiss lake village must have existed from six thousand to seven thousand years ago. By a similar calculation he fixes the date of a settlement (Yverdun) of the transition period at three thousand three hundred years ago. These calculations are generally not regarded as based upon sufficient data; but Sir Charles Lyell, who speaks more favorably of them than any one else, says "they deserve notice, and appear to me to be full of promise."

Calculations from other data arrive at a different result. The settlement of Marin, the distinctive settlement of the iron period, has an entirely distinctive character, altogether the most modern type. When the Emperor Napoleon was preparing his Life of Cæsar, he instituted careful explorations of the site of Alesia, which was taken by Cæsar after a memorable siege. The iron swords found there are identical with the swords found at Marin. Moreover, at this settlement

Of Western Europe.

were found coins of Gaul, of Marseilles, and some Roman coins, one as late as Claudius. This, the latest village, must therefore have lasted till about the Christian era. No rye has been found. Their grains were the small-grained, primitive wheat, and the six-rowed barley. The six-row barley is found upon Italian coin struck about five or six hundred years before Christ. Bronze, wheat, and barley are the distinctive marks of Greece in the times of Hesiod and Homer. As civilization traveled westward, the period of bronze, wheat, and barley must have been later in Switzerland than in Greece. At the settlement of Wauvyl, which belongs to the stone period, and is regarded as one of the oldest, were found glass beads, such as were made in Phœnicia and Egypt, and must have come by means of Phœnician commerce. This settlement must therefore have been in existence as late as fifteen hundred years before Christ. By this calculation, these villages would not extend back more than two thousand years before our era, and this is the limit fixed by Keller, the most careful student of the whole subject.

The nationality of the lake dwellers has been much discussed. The French appear to have settled in the statement or assumption that the inhabitants of the stone age were a primitive race; that the Celts, an Arian race, acquainted with bronze, surging from the East, and filling Western Europe, exterminated the original settlers, took possession of their habitations, and dropped into their mode of life. But, if this were true, the lakes should have some traces of the struggle, and yield human skeletons in attestation of it. Yet, in all the lakes, only five human skulls and few other human bones have been found. There are no traces of sudden change. From first to last the villages appear to have been constructed upon the same plan, and the mode of life in them appears to have been substantially the same. The earliest bronze implements appear to have been cast after the model of those of stone in use, and new forms adopted with increased knowledge of the capabilities of metal. So, too, the earliest iron weapons appear to have been wrought into the shape of bronze castings, and only later advantage was taken of the malleable property of iron. The progress of these people was gradual, and has every indication of having been continuous. Hence, as we know the inhabitants of these villages were, in their latter days, what is called Celtic, we may reasonably infer that the lake settlements were from the first of Celtic origin.

There is, however, one consideration which I have not seen presented, which might be urged in favor of the theory that the introduction of bronze came with a new immigrant race. In many of the settlements have been found horned or crescent-shaped objects, the purpose of which is not known. Mr. Keller plausibly suggests that they were connected with the Druidical worship of the moon. Now, these relics are not found in the earlier settlements of the stone age; they are only found where bronze instruments are also found. If the supposition of Mr. Keller is correct, then these objects tend to indicate the presence of a new religious worship cotemporaneous with the introduction of the use of metal. And the cotemporaneous introduction of both would favor the opinion that they were also cotemporaneous with the incoming of a new race.

Of Western Europe.   15

Groping in the dark for the history of these early people, we can deal only in hypotheses and probabilities. So, as to the period of the abandonment of the pile dwellings, it can only be said that they were probably abandoned gradually. The increasing sense of confinement and discomfort accompanying the development of new wants, which necessarily came with new acquisitions and improvements; or, perhaps, the growth of confidence and security which came with the use of metal weapons, or both together, seem to have led to a gradual abandonment of these habitations. Villages of the stone age are found in all the lakes; villages of the bronze age are found only in the western lakes. And villages where iron is found have been discovered only in two lakes. The whole system seems to have been finally abandoned about the beginning of the present era. Sir Charles Lyell is probably mistaken in saying that such villages existed at Chavanne-and Noville in the sixth century, for they are not named in Sir John Lubbock's later and fuller notice, or in Keller's exhaustive account. But some faint traces have lingered to our day. The fishermen in the Limmat built their huts upon the same plan down to the last century, and in a secluded valley in the Vorder Rhine, where an antique dialect is yet heard, the cattle and sheep and pigs show clear traces of the varieties whose bones are found among the remains of the lake dwellings.

The lake dwellings thus lose much of their mystery. Their buildings differed from their cotemporaries in Western Europe only in the accident of situation. They sought for security in their lakes, as those upon the mainland did upon steep hills. Throughout France,

The Primitive Inhabitants

the British Isles, Germany, and Denmark, the same successive eras of stone, bronze, and iron prevailed. The straight-bladed iron swords, the leaf-like bronze swords, the metal ornaments, and the ruder implements of stone, are found alike in all these countries. The old monuments which have perplexed antiquaries, though still without date in years, range themselves in a certain order of succession. The tumuli take place in the age of bronze, and the barrows in the age of stone. The venerable circle of stonehenge takes its place in history in the age of bronze.

On the Baltic shores of Denmark are remains which belong to a ruder, if not an earlier, epoch. These are simple heaps of oyster-shells, which have received an unpronounceable Danish name, meaning "kitchen refuse." The tribes now living in the Straits of Terra del Fuego and the northern coast of Australia live chiefly on shell fish, and the debris of their repasts accumulate in great masses of shells. So, in former days, lived and fed an oyster-loving tribe on the shores of Denmark. Bones of animals and birds, and occasional stone arrow-heads and hatchets mingled in the heap, have been studied as carefully as the remains found in the lakes. The stone implements are very rude and simple. The bones indicate no domestic animal but a small dog. There are no indications of wheat, barley, or other vegetable food. The bones of deep-sea fish indicate that the people used boats. The different stages of growth of deer's antlers found, indicate that the shores were not a mere summer resort, but were the permanent dwelling-place of an extremely rude people.

The only extinct animal whose bones are found there

Of Western Europe. 17

is the urus. But the oyster is no longer found in the brackish water of the Baltic, and the muscle and other shell-fish now reach there only one-third of the size that is shown in these refuse heaps, and which they still attain in the ocean. But it is known that, at no remote period, ocean currents swept through Denmark in straits now closed, and Sweden has been gradually rising at the rate of two feet in a century in the southern part, and five feet in a century in the north. The shores of Denmark, however, it is said, rise only at the rate of two or three inches per century. If these shores have been rising at the rate of two or three inches per century, the shell heaps are now so near the level of the water that they can not be credited with any antiquity exceeding four thousand years. Hence, though they certainly belong to an earlier type of civilization, there seems no reason for making them chronologically belong to a more remote date than the more advanced races who built the barrows and tumuli. This view is corroborated by the fact that the remains of no extinct animal but the urus are found here.

One circumstance has been seized to give them a more venerable antiquity. Denmark has been covered with beech forest as long as we have any account of it. But trunks of trees found in peat beds show that it was preceded by oak, which in turn was preceded by forests of pine. In a peat bed, under the trunk of a huge pine, which itself lies under superimposed oak and beech, a flint arrow-head has been found. And in the shell heaps are found the bones of a bird (*capercailzie*) which is supposed to have fed on pine buds. So with guessers at the unknown duration of the unknown forests, a remote conjectural antiquity is commonly ascribed to these simple remains.

But it is not in the lake dwellings, or the shell mounds, or the peat beds, that we are to look for the primitive inhabitants of Western Europe. The archæologist indeed goes no further. But the geologist, peering beyond, descries a fossil man. Not every petrifaction, however, is a fossil. We must define what is properly meant by this term.

The forces of nature are still at work ceaselessly changing the surface of the earth. The sea eats away its shores, the waves grind up the fragments, and the currents bear away the debris, deposit it, and form submarine strata. Rivers in like manner washing away the soil of their valleys, create new formations. Volcanoes still scatter their ashes and lava, and dripping caves sheet their floors with stalagmite. The deposits formed by erosion and transportation of currents go by the general name of alluvium. This name, however, is particularly given to the deposits formed by streams flowing in their present beds. The older alluvium, resting directly upon the tertiary strata, some geologists ascribe to a catastrophe different from the operations we now witness, and which they call the diluvium of the north. Hence, they call this old deposit diluvium, and also call the era of its formation the quaternary period. Any remains, therefore, found in the proper alluvium belong to history and archæology. They must be found in the diluvium, or quaternary, to be ranked as fossils.

Other geologists, noting the slow change of level which is still going on in the world—some shores ris-

Of Western Europe.

ing and others sinking—find existing phenomena sufficient, if lapse of time enough is allowed, and designate ages by the nature of the remains found in them. Sir Charles Lyell and others, noticing that different strata of the tertiary formation contain different proportions of extinct and still living species, have divided that formation, accordingly, into three periods—eocene, miocene, and pliocene. Giving the name post-tertiary to all subsequent to the tertiary, they still find in some of the post-tertiary formations remains of animals now extinct. To this portion of the post-tertiary they give the name of post-pliocene. The other, which contains only the remains of animals now existing, they call recent. Hence it is in this formation, by whatever name we call it, whether diluvium, quaternary, drift, or post-pliocene, that the geologist must find human remains before he can show us fossil man.

In the museum in Paris is a petrified skeleton of a woman imbedded in a calcareous rock, found in the island of Guadaloupe. But this rock is still in process of formation. The sea washing up shells, with detritus of the rock of the island, forms a conglomerate, in which all the shells are such as now live on the shore, and the skeleton appears to belong to the Carib tribe, which inhabited the island at a recent date.

In a peat-bog in Sweden was found the skeleton of a bison, bearing marks of a wound made by a hatchet. Near it was found a stone hatchet, which, on being applied, fitted the wound. Close at hand was a human skeleton, the hunter and his prey imbedded together. But the bison is not yet extinct; it still lives in the Lithuanian forest, and peat still grows.

Messrs. Lartet and Christy, great names in these investigations, described, in 1861, the cave of Lombrines, in the Pyrenees, where human bones were found imbedded under stalagmite, which were pronounced cotemporary with the mammoth. But Mr. Garrigou read a paper before the Société d'Anthropologie, in Paris, on the 15th of December, 1864, in which he stated that, upon a subsequent examination of this cave and others in the Pyrenees, by careful scrutiny of the way in which the bones had been washed in through crevices by a stream still running, he became convinced that there was no proof that they were introduced at this early period, but that they should be regarded as cotemporary with the lake dwellings. He added that Lartet, Christy, d'Archiac, Milne Edwards, and others, concurred in this conclusion, and applied it to other caves in the Pyrenees.

But there are cases which can not be so summarily disposed of. Of the animals which lived in the post-pliocene period, some are extinct, though the greater number still survive. To fix man as belonging to that period, it is necessary to show that he was cotemporary with the animals now extinct. This might be done by showing his remains in such juxtaposition with the extinct species as to exclude any hypothesis but the one that they lived together; or else to show human remains naturally inclosed in a deposit which was made at that period. The post-pliocene period was marked by a cold climate in Western Europe. Among the animals now extinct, which flourished then, are the cave bear, cave lion, cave hyena, gigantic Irish elk, the hairy elephant or mammoth, the woolly rhinoceros, the urus or

Of Western Europe.

great ox; to which may be added—as extinct in Western Europe, though still surviving in colder regions—the reindeer. The urus was extinct in Gaul before the campaigns of Julius Cæsar, though it survived in Germany long after. The reindeer must have disappeared then, at a still earlier day, and has been kept alive to this day in Sweden and Norway, only by rigid game laws. The mammoth and rhinoceros appear to have vanished at a still more remote period, as only a few of their bodies have been found in Siberia, incased in ice, which enveloped them before the flesh had begun to decay. Of the cave bear and others we have nothing but fossil remains. Hence, Mr. Lartet, assuming epochs of successive disappearance, divides the post-pliocene age into four periods—those of the cave bear, of the mammoth and rhinoceros, of the reindeer, and of the urus. The proposition is, therefore, to show that man was a cotemporary with the first three of these periods.

The caves of Perigord furnish part of the proofs. These caves have yielded numerous instruments made of reindeer horn. Some fragments appear to have been sawed. One is fashioned into a delicate, fine-pointed needle, with an eye so small it seemed impossible it could be made with the rude implements of those primitive people. But this doubt was removed when Mr. Lartet, with one of the sharp-pointed pieces of quartz, which seemed to have been used as awls, made a puncture as fine. Some of the reindeer horns have designs engraved upon them, representing the deer, elk, ox, boar, and other animals. These are not all mere outline sketches; some are shaded drawings. The most interesting is an unfinished dagger, the handle carved to

The Primitive Inhabitants

represent a reindeer with his head thrown back, his antlers lying along his shoulders, his fore legs drawn under his belly, and hind legs extended along the middle of the blade. The spirit of the design, and the skill with which the natural form of the horn is adapted to it, make it a veritable work of art. All who have seen these objects unite in saying that they obviously were carved from the bones of recently killed animals, not from fossils dug up. In the cave of Eyzies was found embedded in breccia, part of the vertebra of a young reindeer, still perforated with a flint arrow-head, which, unquestionably, penetrated there when the bone was soft. Man was, therefore, cotemporary with the reindeer in Southern France.

Similar evidence connects him with the mammoth. A tusk has been found engraved with the head of two oxen. A piece of ivory has also been exhumed bearing a spirited and unmistakable sketch of a mammoth. The animal having been found entire, frozen in Siberia, his appearance is now known,—not merely from inference from the skeleton, but from actual view. And here is found a portrait taken from life by a man who hunted the mammoth when he ranged the valleys of Southern France. A wood-cut of this can be seen in the February number of the "Salem Natural History Magazine."

The cave of Aurignac, in Upper Garonne, near the Pyrenees, brings man in contact with the cave bear and hyena, as well as the mammoth rhinoceros and reindeer. A peasant working on the highway, near Aurignac, in 1865, noticed that rabbits took refuge in a hole in the hill-side. Putting his hand into the hole one day, he

Of Western Europe. 23

drew out a human bone. He began to remove the earth, and found an upright stone slab. Removing the slab, he found a small cavern nearly filled with human bones. The mayor of Aurignac hearing of it, removed the skeletons, and buried them in the village cemetery. But, being a physician, he first examined them sufficiently to perceive that they were the bones of eighteen persons,—men, women, and children.

Mr. Lartet repaired to the spot as soon as he got wind of the discovery, and made a thorough exploration. He found in the cave a level floor, apparently of made earth, in which were still left a few human fragments. Besides these were a flint knife which had never been used, eighteen perforated disks of shell which had apparently once formed a necklace, a carved bear's tusk, and a few teeth of a lion. He also found the skeleton of a cave bear, the bones lying in such order and juxtaposition as to show that they had been covered with flesh when placed in the cave. These bones were all undisturbed, and suggest that with the quartz and shell and carved bone, they had been left there as a funeral rite with the buried dead. When the earth outside the cave was removed, a hearth of flint sandstone was found, laid upon a smooth surface, excavated underneath. Upon this were evidences of fire. Scattered about were the bones of seventeen animals, including all the extinct species I have named. Many of them were charred by fire and scraped as if by the quartz knife, which had removed the meat. Scattered about were more than a hundred objects of flint, knives, arrow-heads, chips, a flint block from which some of these had been chipped, and one of those pulley-shaped utensils of rough stone, which have so puzzled archæologists, but which the Danish antiquaries take to be implements used in chipping off and forming flint implements. The bones about this fire-place were many of them gnawed by some carniverous beast, the soft ends quite eaten away, and among the ashes were found fossil excrements of the hyena. Here was indubitable evidence that man had eaten the mammoth and rhinoceros; that he had interred a cave bear while the bones were still covered with flesh, and that the hyena had banqueted on the remains of his feast.

In England, in a cave containing bones of those extinct animals, a well-formed flint arrow-head was found lying under the entire leg of a cave bear, all the most delicate bones of which were in position, showing that it had been deposited there when bound together with its ligaments at least, if not covered with flesh. In the cave of Engis, in Belgium, a human skull was found with the same surroundings, imbedded in breccia, under a floor of stalagmite.

The caves are not the only repositories of evidence. Strata of drift, filled with post-pliocene remains, have also yielded stone arrow-heads and hatchets. M. Boucher de Perthes first discovered them in the valley of the Somme, in Northern France. Excavations made to obtain earth for the fortifications of Abbeville, and railway cuttings, gave him ample opportunity to explore this formation. In 1841, he began to collect the implements so found; but all his statements were met with quiet skepticism, or turned off with the remark that his so-called arrow-heads and hatchets were accidental natural forms. He set about collecting all the

Of Western Europe.   25

flints of natural form most resembling them; and the difference between the manufactured and the natural flint was obvious. After years of scientific disdain, one geologist of repute, Dr. Rigollot, of Amiens, visited him, saw at a glance that the collection was of manufactured implements, and, returning to Amiens, explored the same stratum there, and found the same objects of stone.

It was objected that M. Boucher de Perthes might be deceived ; that these implements might be given to him by workmen who falsely pretended to find them *in situ*. He followed the excavations in person, and with his own hands took the hatchets from their beds. It was then objected that they might have sunk through the superincumbent earth to their present position long after the stratum was formed. But the soil was, in its natural state, free from fissure ; the implements were diffused all through the drift, were found from eighteen to thirty feet below the surface, and often found underneath animal fossils.

But the cave discoveries had not yet become rife, and ·M. Boucher de Perthes could not yet find credit. In 1859 a party of leading English geologists visited him, saw his collection, explored the excavations, found the implements there *in situ*, published an account of their visit, and the scientific world at length accepted the facts. The same formation was explored where it exists in England, and with the same result.

Objection still was raised that no human bones had yet been found along with these implements. To this it was answered by Sir Charles Lyell, by Lubbock, and others, that this drift was the deposit of a rapid current, and much compressed by the heavy winter ice of the quaternary period, so that human bones might well have been destroyed; and, besides, that the Swiss lakes and Danish shell heaps were almost devoid of human bones. But, finally, at the meeting of the Société d'Anthropologie, of 13th August, 1864, M. Boucher de Perthes announced that he had found fragments of human bones, representing all ages. Remembering the captiousness which had met his former statements, he had persuaded the mayor and several of the leading men of Abbeville to accompany him to the excavations. stand by the workmen as they dug, and receive with their own hands the human fragments from their bed as they were reached.

Of all the relics found, no others have excited so much interest as the human skulls—one found in the cave of Neanderthal, near Dusseldorf; the other in the cave of Engis, in Belgium. The Neanderthal skull has given rise to unusual discussion. The brain capacity, seventy-five cubic inches, is very near an average between a Hindoo and the largest known healthy European skull. But while the brain capacity is so near an average, the shape and formation are the most brutal of any known human skull. The extraordinary prominence of the superciliary arches, the unparalleled flattening of both the forehead and the occiput, and the straightness of the sutures, make this the most ape-like of human skulls. Learned men who claim to know, say it bears no marks of having been the skull of an idiot, and no marks of artificial compression. The rest of the skeleton has nothing peculiar. The stout-

Of Western Europe. 27

ness of the bones and the development of the muscular ridges show that the man must have had great physical strength. It is, of course, impossible to say whether this remarkable skull was an individual instance, or the ordinary type of some race. It is undoubtedly very ancient, but nothing found in the cave with it, and nothing in the manner in which it seems to have been deposited there, warrants the statement that it is entitled to belong to the post-pliocene period. It may have been cotemporary with the mammoth, but it may be much more recent.

The Engis skull, however, was found so associated with other fossils, that it is accepted as an unquestionable relic of the days of the mammoth and the cave bear. This skull is in no wise peculiar. Its dimensions are almost precisely identical with two modern skulls, one Australian, and one an English skull, noted in Hunterian museum as typically Caucasian. So far as the scanty human fossil remains give indication, the physical structure of man has undergone no change since he first appeared on earth. Like existing animals that have come down from the post-pliocene period, his type remains the same.

During that whole era, man made little advance in civilization in Western Europe. In the last few thousand years, civilization has accelerated in a geometrical ratio. But as we dimly peer into the conjectural past, the advance appears to have been, with occasional fluctuations, more sluggish, till we get back to a uniform degree lasting through cycles. The data we have are certainly scanty. The stone implements then used, so far as yet discovered, are of the ruder type, simply chipped, not polished. No specimens of their pottery have as yet been found. There is nothing yet to show they knew anything of agriculture. At the same time, their carvings became a lost art. During all the period of the lake dwellings, no imitations of leaves, animals, or other natural objects were attempted before the introduction of iron. The attempt, even then, to introduce animal shapes into their ornamentation, showed, in that particular, very great inferiority to the cave dwellers of Perigord. The men of the fossil time, living in caves, undoubtedly were as rude as some savage tribes now living; but their works and their funeral rites show that infant man, a new comer upon the world, dwelling among mammoths and gigantic elks, from the beginning asserted his supremacy over other created beings, and showed himself endowed with intelligence, aspiration for art, and belief in his immortality.

But I am checked in calling this the beginning of man. Certain bones have been lately picked up in Southern France. These bones have scratches upon them. They are the bones of the tropical elephant. The scratches are said to be marks made by a sharp quartz implement in scraping off the meat. Hence it has been intimated that the primitive inhabitants of Western Europe may have been cotemporary with the tropical elephant. This suggestion carries us back to an epoch as remote to the time that we have been considering, as that is to the present day. But the suggestion that man lived then, is based on no discovery of remains of a degraded human type, or of skeleton in-

Of Western Europe. 29

termediate between man and gorilla, but is founded upon the supposed presence among the remains of that day of the traces of human intelligence.*

*The recent discovery by Mr. Calvert of engraved bones in strata of the miocene period, in the Dardanelles, is considered as having established the fact of man's existence as early as the miocene epoch.

DARWINISM AND DEITY.

DARWIN claims to have established the existence of a law of nature, which regulates the progressive appearance on earth of the diversified forms of life. I propose to say a few words about his theory, and to add some suggestions about laws of nature in general.

It is accepted by all, that the first forms of life were the simplest; that higher forms appeared later, and man last of all. Whether we read the written account in Genesis, or try to decipher the fossil record inscribed on the earth's strata, this general statement is equally discerned.

In trying to account for this progressive appearance of diversified forms of life, the most obvious method is, to ascribe it to successive acts of creative power.

This theory of successive creation is upheld by some men of science.

They say that not only was the beginning of the world a creation, but there is reason for holding that the creative power is not in abeyance, but is still in daily exercise. It is said that the spiritual part of man, the soul, the Me, is not an aggregation of particles, but is an absolute, indivisible unit. It is impossible to imagine the consciousness of a person to be divided into separate consciousnesses. But an absolute, indivisible

Darwinism and Deity.

unit, not made up of particles, is itself an ultimate particle, and can not be made from anything else. Hence, the soul of each person, the Me, must be an original creation.

Plato held that the soul of each person, or what he called the spiritual and immortal body, was brought into being by a direct act of creative power; but also maintained that all souls were created in the beginning, and that they transmigrate from body to body.

Now, if we reject the doctrine of transmigration, but agree that the birth of each human soul is an act of direct creation, there arises an antecedent probability that the coming into being of every new form of life, every species, has been due to acts of specific creation.

Men of science have said that this antecedent probability is verified by the facts of geology. It is agreed by all that the earth's surface has undergone great changes; that continents have been submerged, and again elevated.; that arctic and torrid climates have succeeded each other in territories now lying in the temperate zone. And it is said by some that the different superimposed strata indicate that there have been breaks in the continuity of life; that at times some great catastrophe has destroyed all life, leaving only fossil epitaphs; and that new forms of life followed with nothing to generate them, with no way of their coming into being but by a new exercise of creative power.

It is further said that these successive creations are all in harmony with a purpose or design; and that this same purpose or design is exhibited even in certain present phases, as in the progressive stages of the human brain before birth, which resemble successively the brain of various orders of animals from the lower, up.

In the same way, it has been observed that in many animals, including man, there are rudimentary parts which are of no use, but serve only as reminders of earlier and preceding species to which such parts were important,—just as the form of the earliest metal implements (and the form of an implement bears the same relation to the inventor that created things do to the creator) retained peculiarities which were of use in stone implements, though of no use in the new material, metal.

This whole theory, however, is falling, or perhaps has fallen, into disfavor among men of science. The main fact on which it rests as a theory of science, is now said not to exist. It is generally denied that there has been any break in the continuity of life. It is said that the great changes which have visited the earth's surface were not due to catastrophes which destroyed life, leaving a void to be filled by renewed acts of creation ; but were wrought by causes which are still in operation.

Strata are still forming at the bottom of lakes and seas. Rocks are still cracking and crumbling into soil. Hills are washing away ; rivers are still cutting channels, and forming alluvium and deltas. Land is still rising and sinking. Venice has sunk fifteen inches since the Doges' palace was built. Crete has tilted up since the days of the Roman Empire. The ports on its western shore have risen twenty feet out of the water, while the cities on its eastern coast are submerged. The peninsula of Norway and Sweden has been rising and tilting

Darwinism and Deity.

steadily, the southern extremity rising at the rate of two feet; North Cape at the rate of five feet per century. Climates are changing. In the last four centuries there has been a constant increase in the severity of the climate in all the region about the upper part of Baffin's Bay. Deserted habitations of Esquimaux are found in tracts where there are no longer inhabitants. At the same time, the glaciers of Greenland have very largely increased. Some of the glaciers of Switzerland are steadily growing, others diminishing, others alternating. Coral reefs are still forming, volcanoes are still in eruption, and volcanic islands still at times thrust themselves above the surface of the sea. These operations are precisely the same indicated by geology. It is said that give time enough, allow a duration in which a million years will count as a fleeting moment, these operations would produce all the changes that the earth's surface is said to have undergone.

Now, if the world has always gone on as it is now going on, the presumption arises, and this presumption accords with what we know of the phenomena of the universe, that there has always been a certain sequence of events; that every fact of nature is related to and dependent on other facts, and has grown out of facts which preceded it. Hence, it is said that every new form of life, every new animal and plant, has been evolved or developed from already existing species. Darwin claims that this progressive development is determined and regulated by a law of nature, which he has eliminated, and which he calls the law of Selection.

A great many marked varieties of domesticated animals and plants have been produced by the care of man.

Darwinism and Deity.

They have not been produced by manufacture or creation, but by eliminating and perpetuating peculiarities which have naturally appeared in individuals. A horse, a bull, a dog, having some special quality, is carefully mated. The best of his progeny is selected, and carefully mated. The process is repeated till a new variety is introduced. This variety is not a true species, permanent and self-perpetuating; but it lasts as a determinate variety, as long as the supervening care of man preserves it. Now it is conceivable that some natural cause might operate in the same manner as this care of man, and by operating permanently, produce a permanent natural difference, and so create a species.

Among men, hereditary traits are often noticed. A heavy lower jaw has been a feature of the Hapsburg family for centuries. And it is said that the ladies of a certain English ducal family still are distinguished by the beautiful form of the neck, which they inherited from their ancestor, one of the ladies of the court of Charles II.

Besides these minute peculiarities, climate, food, and the other conditions of life affect physical traits. When I was in Colorado a few years ago I was told that the chests of persons and of horses that had lived several years at Georgetown, some 9,000 feet above the level of the sea, had become expanded. The necessity of breathing a larger amount of the rarified air of that elevated region required larger lungs. And persons who follow a calling requiring especial use of particular muscles or organs find those muscles and organs largely develop; while, on the other hand, parts of the body long disused have a tendency to shrink and diminish.

Darwinism and Deity. 35

In the same way, diet and mode of life affect the body. Each nation in Europe has its characteristics, and the American people, though so recent, are already distinguishable from their ancestors.

Now two facts are quite certain. One is, that no two animals, even of the same species, are precisely alike. Every individual has its own peculiarities. The other fact is, that vastly more are born than arrive at maturity. If all animals born reached maturity, the world would soon be heaped up with the crowd. Hence, there is a continual competitive struggle for existence, and in this struggle those mostly survive which are best fitted to survive in the existing conditions of life.

If, for example, various species should migrate to the Arctic regions, the sustenance of animal heat would become a matter of vital importance. White is the color that protects against external heat or cold. Hence, those animals which should happen to have white or nearly white fur would, other things being equal, have the best chance of surviving. Besides, a white-furred animal would be least distinguishable on the snowy surface, and so would have the best chance of escaping from its pursuers, and at the same time, the best chance of coming unperceived upon its own prey. These constant chances operating through cycles would tend to eliminate all dark-skinned animals, leaving only the white to survive. So in animals that trust to speed, either for their own safety, or for overtaking their prey, the swiftest would have the best chance for life, and in long course of ages, the swift-footed of those species would tend to predominate, and the slow to disappear.

So of an insect tribe infesting trees, if one should

36 *Darwinism and Deity.*

happen to be born somewhat resembling the bark of the tree in appearance, it would have a chance of escaping unobserved the birds that snap up its brighter-colored kindred. Of the progeny of this one, such as inherited this peculiarity would have the same chance of preserving life ; and so, in the long course of time, would grow of a species so closely resembling the bark of the tree on which it lived, as to find its safety therein.

In the same way, if any individual should happen to be born with increased facility for securing subsistence, either greater efficiency in obtaining food, or greater capacity for assimilating the food at hand, such individual would have increased chance of surviving in the struggle for life; and its progeny inheriting the same peculiarity would, by having the same chance of surviving, increase the tendency to propagate this peculiarity of structure.

The great changes which the earth's surface has undergone would give greater room for the display of this struggle for life. Change of climate and soil would change vegetation. And this change of the conditions of life would impose new conditions upon the chances of survivorship. It might intensify the chances of the predominating varieties, or it might nullify their chances and give increased chances to some new peculiarity.

Besides the law of survivorship of the fittest, which is called the law of Natural Selection, there is another element, somewhat analogous, called Sexual Selection. The males of certain animals have a contest for the possession of the female. She remains an indifferent spectator, and quietly goes off with the victor. Here the strongest and most agile males have progeny, while

Darwinism and Deity.

the weaker leave no-offspring. Hence there is a tendency to produce a race of strong active males.

In other races, particularly among birds, the female makes her selection. One species is carried away by song. The males exercise all their vocal powers, and the sweetest singer carries away the prize. Another species is attracted by brilliant plumage; and here the lucky male endowed with the brightest feathers succeeds. This course of selection tends in the long lapse of ages to increase the musical power in the one species, and the brilliancy of plumage in the other.

However minute any single variation from existing types might be, it is said that give time enough, time without stint, time without limit, these processes of natural selection, together with the changes of climate and surface, would be sufficient to account for the production of the various diversified forms of life which have appeared since the first were brought into being.

But not only might new forms of life be so produced. It is further said, there are reasons for believing they have been actually so produced.

The fact that new breeds, that new temporary varieties are produced in a short time by superintending human care, raises the presumption that permanent changes of structure, that is, new species, would be produced by natural causes, operating for an indefinite duration in a way analogous to human care.

Some facts strengthen this presumption. For instance: pigs in Florida feed on an herb which rots off the hoofs of all but black pigs. This cause has not been operating long enough to prevent the birth of light or party-colored pigs; but it prevents any but the black

Darwinism and Deity.

from arriving at maturity. Further it is said, that parts that are serviceable in the lower orders of animals are found in a rudimentary state in the higher, as if they had gradually disappeared by disuse. For instance, the *os coccyx* in man is a rudimentary tail. And the puncture in the lower part of the *os humerus*, which is the passage for a nerve in monkeys, is of no use in the human frame. Yet it is found in one per cent. of human skeletons of the present day, and in a larger per cent. of human skeletons three or four thousand years old, in some parts of France.

So far I have offered, not a sketch, but only a rude indication of the general drift of the theory of specific creation and of Darwin's theory of the laws of selection. As to the respective merits and probabilities of these theories, I do not pretend to offer an opinion. *Non nostrum inter vos tantas componere lites.* Men who devote their lives to scientific investigations will toil to a determination, and the world will accept the result.

But there are some suggestions that any of us may make about Darwin's theory. He does not pretend to solve the question, as to the origin of life, or the essence of life, or the power that produces the initial variations in the forms of life which give opportunity for selection. Accepting these, his aim is to ascertain and determine a law by which they produce the permanent forms of life, which we call species.

His theory as to the existence of this law, is gaining ground daily among men devoted to natural science.

But his theory can hardly yet be called " the law " of the development of species. For a true law of nature explaining the phenomena of a certain class, must ex-

Darwinism and Deity.

plain all the phenomena of that class. It can not be accepted as a law of nature, if it be inconsistent with a single fact of nature. And the law of selection confessedly does not explain all the phenomena of the development of species. For Darwin says, there are in man, and other animals, parts which do not appear to be of any present use, or to have ever been of use in any previous form of life. And such parts can not be accounted for by the law of selection.

Further, even so far as the law of selection is consistent with known facts, it can not now be taken as absolutely true, but only as provisionally true. For a larger acquaintance with the facts of nature may show it to be incorrect, and require it to be modified and abandoned. The Ptolemaic theory of the universe was a good scientific theory in its day, for it was consistent with all the facts then known of the heavenly bodies. But a larger acquaintance with the movements of those bodies required that theory to be dropped and supplanted by the Copernican theory.

Finally, although several species have disappeared within the last two thousand years, it is not known that a single new species has appeared since the last fossil era. It must therefore take, so far as we know, thousands of years, to produce any, even the smallest, permanent change in the structure of either animal or vegetable life. But though we thus know that a very long period is necessary, we do not know how much would be sufficient. We have not yet, therefore, attained at anything like a unit of measurement of time required for the workings of Darwin's law.

But late discoveries have shown that the people who

Darwinism and Deity.

lived in southern France when the reindeer and the hairy elephant abounded there, attained not only mechanical skill, but considerable artistic power in carving. The skeletons found in the cave of Engis show that man, just as we see him now, with well-developed skull of the present type, existed in the post-pliocene periods. Indications of man, flint implements made by him, have indeed been found dating back to the still earlier period when the tropical elephant roamed in France. Lyell, speaking of changes in physical geography since those skeletons were washed into the cave of Engis, says, "But although we may be unable to estimate the minimum required for the changes in physical geography above alluded to, we can not fail to perceive that the duration of the period (the post-pliocene) must have been very protracted, and that other ages of comparative inaction may have followed, separating the post-pliocene from the historical periods, and constituting an interval no less indefinite in its duration."

Then if man, the final product, existed fully developed, as we see him now, so early, and we are still unable to estimate the duration required by Darwin's law, to produce even the slightest change of species, it may be that the development from a mollusk up to man, in accordance with Darwin's law, would demand even greater duration than the dizzy cycles allowed by geology for the formation of all the earth's crust.

While men of science are interested in investigating and ferreting out the truths of nature, the world at large are more concerned in the consequences of the researches than in the researches themselves. More people care for an accurate prediction of the weather,

Darwinism and Deity.

than for mere meteorological investigation. The theories and processes of chemistry interest few compared with the number who prize the practical appliances resulting from the studies of chemists. The whole matter of spectrum analysis was ignored by the bulk of mankind as a scientific whim, till it was found to be of service in business.

So it is with any proposition of science which bears upon religious dogma or theological opinion. As these are matters of intense concern, any scientific theory which bears upon such matters is apt in the first place to meet with approval or rejection according to that bearing. Now, the belief is deeply seated in men that God made the world ; that all we see, is His handiwork. And when it is proposed to prove that man, and the beasts of the field, and all trees, were called into being by some law of nature, there is an instinctive feeling, that here is an attempt to withdraw the world from his supervision, and substitute a laboratory in his place. Whether this feeling is well-grounded or not, depends somewhat upon the true meaning of the phrase "laws of nature."

What are the laws of nature? In a general way it may be said they are formulas, expressing the order of succession, and the mode of operation of natural phenomena. The law of light explains the phenomena of light. It says the phenomena of light are produced by the undulations of a subtle ether. The ether is made to undulate by the appearance of a luminous body. A luminous body is one which causes the ether to undulate. It causes the ether to undulate by virtue of some innate force of nature. What is that force of nature?

Darwinism and Deity.

The law of electricity explains the order and succession of electrical phenomena. Electrical phenomena are produced by a natural force called electricity. What is that natural force?

Physical science concerns itself only with phenomena and their order of succession. If we ask what is the nature of the force which produces phenomena, it has no answer.

This can be illustrated farther, by taking a single force of nature; for example, the attraction of gravitation. I remember when in college, Prof. Pierce, the chief of American mathematicians, after going over on the blackboard a demonstration of the theory of universal gravitation, turned to the class, and said: "Here, gentlemen, is a demonstration of that law. We have proved that every particle of matter tends toward every other particle of matter in inverse proportion to the square of the distance, etc. If you ask what makes them so tend, this department has no answer; you must take that question to another department of the university."

Newton had already said substantially the same thing. At the close of the Principia he says: "Hitherto, I have not been able to deduce the *cause* of those properties from phenomena, and I frame no hypothesis; for whatever is deduced from phenomena, is to be called an hypothesis, and hypotheses, whether metaphysical or physical, whether of occult qualities or mechanical, have no place in experimental philosophy. To us, it is enough that gravity does really exist and act according to the rules which we have explained."

If experimental philosophy will not tell us what is this force that we call gravity or attraction of gravita-

Darwinism and Deity. 43

tion, let us recur to another master mind, whose grand intellect was absorbed, not in problems of experimental philosophy, but in fathoming the essence of things.

Newton develops one law, the law of inertia; that is, that matter is not self-moving, but remains at rest till it is moved, and then continues moving in the direction impelled, till it is stopped. Plato also says that matter is inert, and moves only as it is moved. But he considers farther, what is it that causes motion? For instance, in the Phædrus, while proving the immortality of the soul, he says: "And therefore the self-moving is the beginning of motion. But if the self-moving is immortal, he who affirms that self-motion is the very idea and essence of the soul will not be put to confusion, for the body which is moved from without is soulless; but that which is moved from within has a soul, and this is involved in the nature of a soul."

Holding that all motion, that is, all force, is simply the exercise of a spiritual being, when he comes, in the Timæus, to explain the origin and creation and operation of the universe, he accounts for the forces and motions of nature, by holding that the universe is a living being. As the spiritual must precede the corporeal, Plato says, "God first created the universe, a spirit, a soul;" then adds, "Now, when the Creator had framed the soul according to his will, he formed within the mind the corporeal universe, and brought them together and united them centre to centre. The soul, interfused everywhere from centre to the circumference of heaven, of which she is the external envelopment, herself turning in herself, began a divine begin-

Darwinism and Deity.

ning of never-ceasing and rational life, enduring through all time."

Plato, then, as the result of the reflections of his life, held that all the motions in nature, that is, all natural phenomena, are caused directly by a spiritual being which pervades the universe. Hence, it follows that what we call the forces of nature are only the will and direct action of that spirit.

Now what is, or rather, who is, the spiritual being that pervades all space? There can be but one answer, and we can give it in the words of Newton.

The very paragraph preceding the one in which he says, experimental philosophy does not pretend to say what gravity is, but only how it acts, is a statement of the government of the universe; and he wrote to Bentley that he put this paragraph into the Principia as an addition and mere hint, which others may develop. He says: "God is omnipotent, not virtually only, but also substantially. In Him are all things contained and moved. It is allowed by all that the Supreme God exists necessarily; and by the same necessity He exists always, and everywhere. Whence, also, He is all similar, all eye, all ear, all brain, all arm, all power to perceive, to understand, to act, but in a manner not at all human, in a manner not at all corporeal, in a manner utterly unknown to us."

Plato says what we call the forces of nature is only the direct action of a spiritual being who pervades the universe, enveloping every particle of matter. And Newton adds, that being is the living God.

The last grand generalization of science, the correlation of forces and the indestructibility of force, does not in any way affect this statement. It is true that force in nature is sometimes in active operation, sometimes apparently latent; is manifested successively in gravitation, cohesion, affinity, electrical attraction and repulsion, heat, etc., and the aggregate of force in the universe is never increased, never diminished, but remains continually the same. But whether we suppose this force to be a quality inherent in matter, or to have been imparted to the universe at its original creation, or to be the continual action of the omnipotent being who envelops every particle in the universe, is a matter wholly indifferent to physical science. Its investigations and inductions are equally consistent with either hypothesis. It is not within the scope of physical science to determine which is true.

It is quite supposable that in time, or at least in eternity, the Omnipotent might lay aside this universe, like shifting a scene, and introduce new orders of being and new natural laws.

Let the imagination penetrate to the faintest nebulæ, to the remotest indications of matter, and as far beyond as its wearied pinions can soar; yet a sphere embracing all it can guess at would be but a speck in infinite space. And it is supposable that beyond there may be even now other universes unlike this, where other forms of being, and a different natural system may prevail; where gravitation and electricity are unknown.

But such speculative possibilities are outside of the domain of physical science. They have nothing to do with it; it has nothing to do with them. It is concerned only with what is actually going on in this

Darwinism and Deity.

universe, with what has happened, and with what will happen so long as it shall last.

When, therefore, we use the phrase, "The Laws of Nature," we only use a convenient form of speech for generalizing what we see of the operations of the universe; and a phrase often first cloaks a fact, then smothers it. But if Plato and Newton are right in their perception of those things which they specially perceived best, the laws of nature, in truth, are only statements of our perceptions of God's continued work. Hence, as a matter of theological concern, it matters not whether new species are brought into being by what we call "specific creation," or by what we call "the laws of nature." In either case it is equally immediately God's own act.

One further remark will be all. Many scientific theories, when first broached, have to encounter not only arguments, but also prejudices.

Darwin's law is no exception. It is, indeed, at first view, at all events, sadly at war with our notions of the dignity of human nature. When Shakespeare says: "What a piece of work man is! How noble in reason! How infinite in faculties! In form and moving how express and admirable! In action how like an angel! In apprehension how like a God!" And when the Psalmist sings, "What.is man, that Thou art mindful of him? and the son of man, that Thou visitest him?

"For thou hast made him a little lower than he angels, and hast crowned him with glory and honor.

"Thou madest him to have dominion over the

Darwinism and Deity.

47

works of Thy hands ; Thou has put all things under his feet," every heart responds.

Hence, we recoil from Darwin's statement : " We thus learn that man is descended from a hairy quadruped, furnished with a tail and pointed ears, probably arboreal in its habits, and an inhabitant of the Old World. This creature, if its whole structure has been examined by a naturalist, would have been classed among the Quadrumana, as surely as would the common and still more ancient progenitor of the Old and New World monkey. The Quadrumana and all the higher mammals are probably derived from an ancient marsupial animal, and this, through a long line of diversified forms, either from some reptile-like, or some amphibian-like creature, and this again from some fish-like animal. In the dim obscurity of the past, we can see that the early progenitor of all the Vertebrata must have been an aquatic animal, provided with branchiæ, with the two sexes united in the same individual, and with the most important organs of the body (such as the brain and heart) imperfectly developed. This animal seems to have been more like the larvas of our existing marine ascidians, than any other known form."

But when the first feeling of disgust abates, two suggestions present themselves. While it is true, there must be a difficulty in determining at what period of such a course of development man appeared with an immortal and responsible soul, it is equally true, that in the case of every individual man we are unable to say just at what time a soul was united to the body.

The other suggestion is this : The theory of Darwin

48 *Darwinism and Deity.*

is based on the supposition that each step of positive improvement grows out of a struggle with the conditions of life, in which the worthy succeed, and in which each success is only a terrace and coin of vantage for further progress. And further, if a mere senseless shell-fish can struggle up through diversified forms to such a being as man, what glorious visions of greatness yet to be attained does not the fact suggest!

The sum of these remarks, then, is this: Darwin does not propose to explain the origin and essence of life. He assumes that simple forms of animal life were originally created with certain powers and capabilities. He proposes to explain the manner in which more complex forms have since appeared. He claims that the action and reaction of these powers and capabilities, and of the conditions of life on each other, constitute a law of nature, which he calls the law of selection, and that all the diversified forms of life which have appeared on earth since the origin of life, have come into existence in accordance with this law.

This theory, however, can not as yet be accepted as a demonstrated law since there are confessedly phenomena which it does not account for.

Further, so far as it is consistent with actual phenomena, it can not be accepted as absolutely true, but only as provisionally true. For if true according to the present state of human knowledge, a larger acquaintance with the phenomena of nature may overthrow it, and require some new theory.

And further, as the development of no new species has ever yet been actually observed, there is no means of determining the duration of time required to produce,

Darwinism and Deity. 49

in accordance with his theory, the slightest permanent variation in the forms of life. And as man, fully developed, existed at least in the later fossil period, his theory may require a greater immensity of time than is allowed by geology for entire formation of the earth.

And, in fine, if the law of selection be a true law of nature, yet it and all the laws of nature are only formulas, expressing human apprehensions of the way in which the Creator carries on the universe.

SOME CONSIDERATIONS ON THE MOUND BUILDERS.

THE first explorers of this valley were surprised to find in the solitudes of the wilderness, overgrown with ancient forests, huge earthworks, concerning which the Indians had not even a tradition. Interest being once aroused, these works have become the object of great examination and much study.

They have been found over a large part of the Mississippi Valley. They are so numerous that Ohio alone is estimated to contain some thousands, large and small. They vary greatly in magnitude. Some are trifling embankments scarcely rising above the surface of the ground, or little hillocks three or four feet high ; while others, like the works of Newark and Portsmouth, in this State, embrace fourteen and sixteen miles of embankment; or, like the mound at Cahokia, Illinois, have a base of six acres, a summit platform of five acres, and a height of ninety feet, containing twenty million cubic feet of earth.

They vary as greatly in design as in size. The purpose of some is obvious; the intention of others has not yet been divined. Some are fortifications; some lookouts or signal stations. Some, filled with bones, are clearly burial mounds. The large conical mounds

Some Considerations on the Mound Builders. 51

have been the subject of much speculation. The late Dr. Wilson, of Newark, told me he believed they were raised gradually by successive burials; that a layer of bodies or skeletons was covered with earth; that, after some time, upon this was placed another layer of bodies covered with earth; and by such repetition the mound grew. Since then, Governor Hayes, who was present at the opening of the great mound at Miamisburg, told me that it was marked by a stratification of earth, with an appearance of vegetable mold between the layers. The same appearance was noted, according to the account in the American *Pioneer*, at the removal of the large mound that formerly stood in this city. And in the exploration of the Gravecreek mound, besides this stratification, the soil appeared mottled, as if by the decay of perishable substances inclosed in it. The same stratified appearance is described in the appearance of similar mounds in Squire and Davis' work, and in Pickett's history of Alabama. In some mounds, perhaps more recent, fragments of bones are found in the layers. This appearance is so uniform that it is, I think, safe to agree with Dr. Wilson, in ascribing the large conical mounds to a gradual accretion by successive burials.

There is another class, sometimes circular, more often rectangular, having flat summits. These are called *truncated* mounds, when the height is considerable; *terraces*, when the surface is large compared with the height. These always have a graded ascent to the summit, frequently one on each side.

These appear to have been constructed for the purpose of having an elevated platform. This may have

52   Some Considerations on the Mound Builders.

been for the residence of chiefs, or for the elevation of temples, or for the performance of public rites.

Others are long rectangular inclosures, apparently places for public games or sports.

Others comprise a vast series of embankments; circles, squares, connecting avenues, and other geometrical figures, as surprising by the precision of their outline as by their magnitude. At these, conjecture is baffled.

Others again are simply raised figures of men, animals, birds, reptiles, on a gigantic scale. Here, too, even guessing fails.

From the predominance of mounds in these structures, their unknown architects, long since extinct, are called the Race of the Mound Builders. They left no history but their works. The Indians who lived in the last two hundred years knew nothing, and say the tribes who preceded them knew nothing of them. If we would learn their history we must appeal to the works themselves.

The study that has been bestowed upon them is not wholly without result. What I have to say of their builders will be grouped under the following heads: Where did they live? When did they live? How did they live? Who were they? What became of them?

Upon all these points, except the last, something can be said that is not pure guess-work.

WHAT ARE THE WORKS?

The first step is to determine what are the works of this distinct race—to eliminate mounds thrown up by the present race of Indians. The groups of small mounds about four feet high about the Minnesota river, have been determined to be mere ruins of the earth-covered huts of the Iowas, who formerly lived there. Excavation has found the charred remains of the tent-poles, remnants of utensils, and sometimes human bones. The Choctaws used to preserve the skeletons of the dead, until they became numerous, and then lay them in a heap on the ground, and cover them with earth, making a small mound. The numerous small mounds in Oregon are similar in appearance, and probably in character. The Sioux sometimes bury a body on a plain, heap billets of wood over the place; and the dust of the prairies, mingling with the decaying wood, makes a small hillock, which is increased by the growth of rank vegetation. In special cases mounds twelve feet high have been erected over noteworthy graves, as over the grave of Blackbird, the Maha chief, —as related by Lewis and Clark; and one over a young brave, near the red pipe-stone quarry, described by Catlin. The recently deserted villages of the Ricarees and Mandans, on the Missouri, were described by Lewis and Clark as being distinguishable, at some little distance, by the encircling embankment, which had been the base of their stockade defense. The earthworks in Central and Western New York, which were at first attributed by Squire to the Mound Builders, have been ascertained by his subsequent careful examination to be partly remains of the stockaded forts used by the Iroquois last century and the present century. And those that are shown to be older, by the heavy forest growths on them, are identical in structure and size.

The small earthworks along the southern shore of

Some Considerations on the Mound Builders.

Lake Erie, all having a military character, were first observed by Colonel Whittlesey to differ from the important works in Southern Ohio, in being smaller, simpler, and having less elevation. The embankment is so slight that it would be useless as a defense, and could have been useful only as the base of a stockade. These might have been small frontier outposts of the mound builders, or might have been the stronghold of some Indian tribe, like the Eries, who lived there till they were exterminated, about 1650, by the Iroquois. The small mounds in Ohio, Indiana, and Kentucky, that are found to be full of human bones, might possibly be the work of Indian tribes, who buried their dead in the manner of the Choctaws.

Discarding these, the territory occupied by works which could not have been built by Indian tribes, such as we know, is well defined. At the south they begin in Eastern Texas, and extend eastward to the Atlantic. Between the western border of the Mississippi and the Alleghanies they extend northward to the Ohio Valley, north of the river, and up into Wisconsin; and, sparsely, across the Mississippi into Minnesota. They are found, also, on the upper Missouri.

Lewis and Clark describe an important work on the bank of the Missouri, where the northern boundary of Nebraska now lies; and A. Barrand, in a paper in the Smithsonian octavo for 1870, describes many in Dakota Territory on the right bank of the Missouri, and the streams flowing into it, up to the Yellowstone. The main locality is, therefore, between the western borders of the Mississippi river and the Alleghany Mountains. The works are not of uniform character throughout

Some Considerations on the Mound Builders.

this region. In the southern tier of States they are, for the most part, large truncated mounds and raised platforms of earth, generally with graded ascents, and frequently in groups.

In the Gulf States there are but few works of a military character. They are scarcely found out of Georgia. One in Fayette, in Mississippi, represented by figure 2, plate xxxviii, in Squire and Davis' work, published by the Smithsonian Institute, has the appearance of a European work. Its outline is the tracing of a bastion of a regular fortification. The account mentions the freshness of its appearance, and the still preserved sharpness of the angles. Now, in the French campaign against the Chickasaws in May, 1736, D'Artaguette remained eleven days in a camp in that neighborhood while waiting to hear of Bienville, and then, leaving his baggage in the camp, marched out to attack the nearest Chickasaw village. I am inclined to consider this work an intrenchment about D'Artaguette's camp. But if the position of this camp was, as stated in Pickett's History of Alabama, a few miles east of Pontotoc, then the work is in just about the position where Montcherval encamped when coming up with reinforcements. In any event, this work appears to be a French field work of their campaign of 1736, not a work of the Mound Builders.

In Georgia are several works of a military character, described by Mr. Jones in his Antiquities of the Southern Indians. All but one near Macon are unimportant. And on the Wateree, in South Carolina, are some defensive works.

In Tennessee, besides the conical, truncated, and terrace mounds, defensive works are not uncommon. One of them at Savannah, on the Tennessee river, is so peculiar that I shall speak of it separately at the close of this paper. In Kentucky, fortifications mingle with the simple mounds. In Central and Southern Ohio every description of work is found, some of them peculiar to this section. In Indiana and Illinois the remains are not so numerous, but the one at Cahokia, Illinois, is the giant of mounds. In Wisconsin there are no fortifications; the inclosed work at Aztalan is not of a military character. Conical mounds are found; but the distinctive feature is the effigy mounds which dot the surface of the State, as if the ancient race had used this region, when it was a prairie, as a vast parchment whereon, by the picture-writing of these effigies, they inscribed their history. On the upper Missouri are found conical mounds and fortifications.

The northern portion of the region inhabited by the Mound Builders is, therefore, the fortified region. The works of defense are found in Tennessee, Kentucky, Ohio, along the upper Missouri, and on the frontier between the Alleghanies and the ocean.

WHEN DID THEY LIVE?

As to the time when the Mound Builders lived, there has been much discussion. From the fact that in the Ohio Valley these works are not observed in the lowest or last-formed river-bottoms, but only on the second and higher lands, the deduction has been drawn that they lived before the rivers had cut their present channels—before the lowest alluvium was formed. But in one case, at least—in the works at Portsmouth—the

Some Considerations on the Mound Builders. 57

lines of embankment were carried on to the lowest bottom, down to the river bank. Colonel Whittlesey wrote to me that high water sometimes flowed against and along these embankments. And at Piqua, while most of the works are on the second and third terraces, a portion—a walled avenue, or covered way—extended to the very water's edge. In general, the works are found just where people build now, on ground above the reach of freshets, leaving the lower ground for tillage. Moreover, all the bones found in the mounds belong to animals that lived in Ohio when it was first visited by Europeans.

In the South, where, however, the rivers have not the same geological history, large works are found on the river banks. The great mound on the Etowah stands on the river bottom surrounded by a ditch, through which water flowed at high stages of the river. One of the mounds on the Wateree, in South Carolina, stands on land subject to overflow. And Bartram conjectured that a series of works which he discovered on the Savannah, were built as places of refuge in times of high water. The indications, therefore, are, that when the Mound Builders lived, the river channels and river bottoms were already formed as they now are.

Another theory has been recently started to prove an extreme antiquity for the mounds. The Cincinnati *Medical News*, for January of this year, gives a resumé of a paper read by J. W. Foster, LL. D., before the Dubuque meeting of the American Association for Science. He speaks of finding " three frontal bones in the Kennicott mound, near Chicago, the only part of the skeletons capable of preservation. The plates were extraordinarily thick ; the superciliary arches were massive, standing out like ropes ; the frontal bones of great strength and sloping backward, encroaching on the parietals, and giving origin to a low forehead." Assuming these skulls to have belonged to Mound Builders, that this was the natural shape, and that these were typical skulls, he inferred that the Mound Builders differed in their physical structure from the Indians, and were a race of low intellect, but mild, inoffensive, easily held in subjection, and easily conquered.

The abstract of this paper, as given in the Cincinnati *Medical News*, does not state in what part of the mound these skulls were found. Yet, as the Indians frequently buried their dead in existing mounds, it is always a matter of first importance to know whether objects found in these structures were placed there by the original builders, or were subsequently inserted by a disturbance of the surface.

A skeleton found on the natural surface of the ground, or near it, under the centre of a mound, can be taken as an original interment ; while one found near the surface, on the sloping sides, must be considered a subsequent intrusion, a burial by the Indians.

Very few skulls that can be certainly attributed to the Mound Builders have been found which did not crumble on being taken out. It is only when the character of the soil or the circumstances of the interment have kept the bones thoroughly dry that any such have been found. Lapham says that only one such has been recovered in Wisconsin. All skulls now preserved that indubitally belong to the Mound Builders, and all that are with strong probability referred to them, are well

Some Considerations on the Mound Builders. 59

developed, well rounded. The best authenticated of all, the one discovered by Squire and Davis, and now No. 1,512 in the collection of the Academy of Natural Science of Philadelphia, is the largest and best formed. It has an internal capacity of ninety cubic inches.

The "frontal bones" of the Kennicott mound may have another origin. The custom of flattening the forehead was common to many Indian tribes. It was the usage of the Choctaws one hundred years ago, and fifty years earlier, Du Pratz says it was the practice of many tribes in the South. No. 1,455, in the Philadelphia collection, a skull artificially flattened, was taken from an intrusive burial in a mound in Alabama, on the shore of Perdido Bay. The mound is thirty feet high. The skull was found near the summit, and a few feet under the surface.

So far as can be judged from the abstract of Dr. Foster's paper, therefore, the deduction that the frontal bones which he describes are remains of the Mound Builders at all is hasty. The assumption that they represent the normal type of the skull is wholly unwarranted, and in conflict with established facts. If they really are remains of the Mound Builders, the inference would be that they were an abnormal formation, a deformity, or else that some of the Mound Builders, like some of the later Indians, adopted the usage of flattening the skull. Indeed, in the recently published Antiquities of Southern Indians, by C. C. Jones, there is an account of a skull found in Georgia which undoubtedly belonged to the Mound Builders, which is artificially flattened.*

---

*Artificial compression was not the cause. Dr. Foster says, in his very valuable work, the " Prehistoric Races of the United

60 *Some Considerations on the Mound Builders.*

Another ground on which the great antiquity of the mounds is supported, is the absence of tradition concerning them among the Indians. But it is only fair to remember that their traditions are mostly worthless; that at best they extend back but a short period; and that the Indians were migratory. Ohio, Kentucky, and

States," published since this paper was read, that he has but one skull showing signs of artificial compression, and that was found in Indiana. He claims in this book to have discovered a special type of crania, which he calls the skull of the Mound Builder: a type so distinct that it must have belonged to a wholly distinct race; a type so degraded that it must have belonged to a very early stage in the development of man.

This theory is based upon nearly a dozen skulls and fragments in his possession. Four of them were taken by Dr. Harper from the works near Merom, Indiana; one came from a mound at Dunleith, Illinois, opposite Dubuque; the rest were found near Chicago.

The statement as to these remains would be more satisfactory if it were more definite as to the precise condition in which they were found. It appears from Mr. Putnam's paper in the fifteenth volume "Proceedings of the Boston Society of Natural History," that besides the mounds, there are, at Merom, also some stone graves, made by placing thin slabs on edge along the sides and ends, and covering with flat stones; and that Dr. Harper took three skeletons from these stone graves. Now, graves of this form are not uncommon near the Ohio, Cumberland, and Tennessee rivers. But this form of burial is so unlike the mound burial that it seems to be the usage of a people different from the nation that constructed the mounds. And not only different, but also more recent. For, as a rule, the skeletons found in these superficial, slightly covered graves are in much better preservation than those buried under the mounds. Moreover, skeletons in some of these graves, in those near Nashville, bear marks of a disease introduced by the whites (Jones' Antiquities of Southern Indians, p. 222). And, in fine, the Indians used this mode of

Some Considerations on the Mound Builders. 61

Middle Tennessee were wholly uninhabited in the latter half of the seventeenth century. Though it is commonly stated that De Soto visited the Cherokees, I do not find the statement supported by the original narratives of De Soto's expedition. The Creeks and Alabamas arrived in the Southern States later than De

burial down to the present century, in Illinois (Ib., p. 220).' It would, therefore, be of some interest to know whether the skulls from Merom, described by Dr. Foster, were taken from the mounds, or were those taken from the stone graves.

The skulls and fragments found near Chicago were dug from little mounds—the loam of the prairie heaped up two and a half feet high. The Indians sometimes heaped such mounds over their dead. And Dr. Foster indeed says, that some of these very mounds were the burying-places of Indians and half-breeds.

As for the skull found at Dunleith, three were taken from a mound there twelve feet high. Of two, we have no information. The third, the one described by Dr. Foster, was buried two feet under the surface, in a grave made of wood and stone. This was obviously not an original, but an intrusive interment; and therefore, according to all accepted inference, was the grave, not of a Mound Builder, but of a modern Indian.

There is nothing in Dr. Foster's statement, therefore, that shows these crania to be relics of the Mound Builders; and their form, as he describes it, is the form of the skull of an Indian idiot.

Other investigators have been very careful in determining the character of interments. Squire and Davis, in all their researches, found but one preserved skull which they could say was certainly that of a Mound Builder. This was found on the natural surface of the ground, under the centre of a mound that was covered by the primitive forest, one of the Chillicothe system of mounds. The skeleton was surrounded by burnt debris, covered by a sheet of mica, and the soil of the mound was clay, impervious to water, and had evidently not been disturb-d. Dr. Lapham, in his exhaustive examination of the mounds of Wisconsin, found only one skull which, by similar indications, he could cer-

62   *Some Considerations on the Mound Builders.*

Soto's time.   The absence of tradition among the Indians, therefore, does not prove much ; and the Indians whom De Soto found, used the truncated mounds so habitually as an elevated base for the dwellings of the chiefs, that it was taken for granted they were the work of the Indians.   Indeed, one of the narrators, Garcilaso de la Vega, describes their manner of constructing them.

But some indication of the age of these monuments is afforded by the forest growth which covers them. Dr. Hildreth said a tree eight hundred years old was felled on one of the mounds at Marietta.   Squire and Davis say trees six hundred years old stood on the fort on Paint creek, west of Chillicothe.   Mr. Barrandt says he observed a tree six hundred years old upon one

---

tainly attribute to the people that constructed the mounds. Another, found in Tennessee, was determined by similar proof. Another was taken from a chamber in the centre of the Grave Creek mound.

These completed the list of certainly authenticated Mound Builders' skulls.   As to these, Dr. Foster simply says they are not like the type that he calls the Mound Builders' skull, but resemble the crania of Indians, and therefore are not of the Mound Builders   But Mr. Jones, in Georgia, has, with the same exactitude, identified one more skull (Antiquities of Southern Indians, p. 160), and to this Dr. Foster will have to make the same objection.   And Dr. Jeffreys Wyman, of Harvard, as cited in Dr. Foster's book, speaking of twenty-four crania sent to him by the late S. S. Lyon, of Kentucky, as skulls of the Mound Builders, says, " A comparison of these crania with those of *the other and later Indians*, show that they have some marked peculiarities, though they are better appreciated when the two kinds are placed side by side, than from any table of measurement or verbal description."

Some Considerations on the Mound Builders. 63

of the works upon the upper Missouri. These are, I believe, the oldest that have been observed.

Many two hundred and four hundred years have been noted. In many cases the forest appears more recent. Judge A. H. Dunlevy, of Lebanon, in a letter to the Historical Society in this city, said that he had noted in the woods upon Fort Ancient an entire absence of the little hillocks, formed by earth about the roots of a tree that is blown down and uprooted. When the tree decays, the uprooted soil forms a knob or hillock, and such are always seen in old forests. From their absence he infers that the woods upon Fort Ancient are the original growth. Professor Lapham made the same observation, and drew the same inference as to forest growth covering a great part of the remains in Wisconsin. The very aged trees, six hundred or more years old, found on some mounds are, then, probably the survivors of the original forest growth on those mounds, and had attained respectable maturity while other mounds were still bare. No long interval would elapse after the abandonment of the earthworks before trees would spring up. Making full allowance for this interval, and for the growth and disappearance of preliminary weeds and shrubs, the forest growth does not indicate an abandonment of any of the mounds at a period more remote than a thousand years, and many of them may have been occupied or used by their builders up to a much later date. The extinction or disappearance of the Mound Builders may, therefore, reasonably be said to have begun about a thousand years ago, and to have been gradual, and not to have been completed until near the discovery of the continent by Columbus.

HOW THEY LIVED.

In considering next how the Mound Builders lived, it is not to be supposed that this race constituted one nation, or one empire. There is no greater similarity in their works, as found in different parts of the country, than in the habits of the multitudinous Indian tribes that subsequently inhabited the same region. Indeed, it may be that several distinct tribes dwelt in this State. One tolerably compact body filled the valleys of the two Miamis and Mad River. Another compact body filled the Scioto Valley. The country between seems not to have been inhabited, but only roved over by hunters. Moreover, the extensive and complex works, of geometrical design, that abound in the Scioto Valley, are scarcely found on the Miamis. The indications, therefore, are that these valleys were the homes of two separate tribes.

The race of Mound Builders must have been a numerous people. While Indiana, Illinois, and Iowa seem to have been sparsely settled by them, the rest of the country must have been thickly peopled along the rivers. In Ohio, for example, they had large settlements on the Ohio at Cincinnati, Portsmouth, and Marietta. On the Scioto, besides Portsmouth, at Chillocothe and Circleville. In the interior were large settlements in the neighborhood of Athens, Worthington, Xenia, Springfield, Dayton, Miamisburg, Hamilton, Oxford, and Eaton. In this county, besides their chief town at Cincinnati, they lived on the Little Miami at Columbia, Plainville, and all along the valley from below Newtown to above Milford; in the interior of the county at Norwood and Sharon; on the Ohio at Sedams-

Some Considerations on the Mound Builders.

ville and Delhi; and on the Great Miami at the mouth of the river at Cleves, and for miles along its banks about Colerain.

This race must have differed in character and mode of government from the modern Indians. The construction of their great earthworks required a species and amount of labor that the Indians would not have submitted to. And the method of the systems of works in Ohio is quite as striking as the character of any single work.

Along the Miami rivers are dotted small mounds on projecting highlands, which seem to have been built to carry intelligence by signals along the valleys. And by the mound at Norwood, signals could be passed from the valley of Millcreek to the Little Miami Valley, near Newtown, and, I believe, to the valley of the Great Miami, near Hamilton. A chain of mounds can be partially traced from the old Cincinnati mound to the fort at the mouth of the Great Miami; and Judge Cox, who is better acquainted than any one else with the works in this country, says the chain is complete. Squire and Davis says there is a series of signal mounds along the Scioto, across Ross county, extending down into Pike and Pickaway. Mr. Sullivant, of Columbus, told me that he once traced a series of signal mounds along the Scioto, from Dublin, entirely across Franklin county, to Pickaway; and added he had no doubt, though he had not verified it by his own observations, that the chain was so continuous that a signal could be instantaneously flashed from the lines of Delaware county to Portsmouth. The controlled labor required to build the separate works, and their systematic combination, seem to

66   *Some Considerations on the Mound Builders.*

indicate that these tribes had a strongly centralized, if not despotic, government.

Living, as they did, in great numbers exclusively along the rich river valleys, this race must have been an agricultural people. There are no traces of their having had any domestic animals; but bones in some of the mounds show that they hunted game.

They had some engineering skill. The extensive works of geometrical outline, in the Scioto Valley, squares, octagons, circles, ellipses, often combined together, are executed with such precision that they must have had some means of measuring angles. It would be no mean task for our engineers to construct them on such a scale with equal exactitude. And the number of the squares that measure exactly one thousand and eighty feet on each side show that they had some standard of measurement.

Their dwellings have disappeared, leaving no trace, unless the flat mounds with graded ascents, as at Marietta, were platforms whereon stood a temple and the chief's house, as like mounds were used in the South three hundred and thirty years ago; and unless the small circular embankments are the crumbled remains of mud walls surrounding dwellings of the people, like the huts of the Mandans in the Northwest.

Their pottery was superior in manufacture and in tasteful design to the ordinary pottery of the Indians.

Their stone pipes, even of the simplest form, like the one in the Historical Society collection in this city, has a certain artistic feeling which is lacking in the pipes of the modern Indian. Some of those found by Squire and Davis have very spirited representations of birds and

Some Considerations on the Mound Builders. 67

animals carved in hard stone. They carved many stone implements or ornaments, the purpose of which can not now be determined. Considerable skill was used in the drilling of tubes of hard stone. Their stone hatchets, axes, arrow-heads and lance-heads were of the same character with those of the Indians. I have not been able to learn that there is any means of distinguishing between them; but in looking over the large collection of the Smithsonian Institution, it appeared to me that those found in the region where the Mound Builders lived were in general of more elaborate design and more careful finish than those found in the Atlantic States, north of South Carolina.

They made a limited use of metals. They had, however, no knowledge of the reduction of ores, or of melting and casting metal. They used hematite simply as a hard stone, and native copper and silver as a malleable stone. Of hematite, they made small wedges or chisels, and plummets, that some suppose were used in weaving. Native copper from Lake Superior was hammered into hatchets, spear-heads, knives, and into various rude ornaments. Native silver, also, probably from Lake Superior, has been found in extremely small quantities, hammered into leaf and wrapped around small copper ornaments.

A few traces of coarse woven cloth have been supposed to be discovered.

Though these people had nothing amounting to commerce, still there was a certain amount of enterprise, and a certain amount of intercourse among the tribes. The copper deposits on both the northern and southern shores of Lake Superior were mined. The shafts they opened, the rude stone hammers they used, blocks of copper they separated from the mass but found too heavy to be removed, remain witnessess of their toil. But the shores of Lake Superior were not inhabited. Hence the residents of Ohio must have made summer expeditions even to the north shore of the lake; and to make a summer expedition productive, they must have gone in working parties of some size. Possibly the earthworks along the southern shore of Lake Erie were fortified camps of these parties. That the crude native copper was brought to Ohio, and then hammered into implements, appears from the fact that lumps of it are found in mounds and under the soil. The implements so made found their way to distant points. They are occasionally found in Southern mounds.

At the same time, bits of obsidian, very few, indeed, but which must have come from Mexico, have been found in Ohio. And some of the pipes found by Squire and Davis indicate that they were made at a distance, or else by persons who had traveled : for one represents a seal ; another a manito, which inhabits on the coast of Florida ; and one represents a toucan feeding from a hand, and the toucan was mentioned by the early Spanish discoverers as the only bird tamed by the Indians.

In fine, the Mound Builders appear to have been an agricultural people, as well as hunters, capable of patient toil, living under a strongly centralized or despotic government, and were somewhat more advanced than the Indians, who succeeded them, in the rudiments of civilization. They were perhaps on a level with the Zuni or Pueblo Indians of Arizona.

WHO WERE THEY?

So far, I have spoken of the Mound Builders, sometimes as distinguished from the Indians, sometimes as distinguished from the modern Indians, so as not to foreclose in advance the discussion of the question which comes next—who were they? Since comparative philology developed into science, the aboriginal American dialects have been subjected to exhaustive study. After a discussion lasting many years, it has been determined that all the languages and dialects between the Esquimaux, on the north, and the straits of Terra del Fuego on the South, differ wholly from the languages of the other continents; and that while they differ widely among themselves in vocabulary, some not having a single word in common with others, they still have all the same organism or character. They all belong to one family, have a common origin. As the formation of a single language is a matter of time, the multitudinous languages found among the Indians of North and South America prove that this family has lived here for a very long period.

The study of the physical structure, as exhibited by their skeletons, has ended in the same result. The skulls of all nations south of the Esquimaux, ancient and modern—Patagonian, Peruvian, Aztec, Mound Builders, and the Indian of the present day —are said by Morton (and his views, though ably questioned by Dr. Wilson, of Toronto, are generally accepted) to present the same type, to constitute one family. Though occasional natives of other continents may in the lapse of years have drifted to the shores of America, they left no trace in the language or the physical struc-

Some Considerations on the Mound Builders.

ture of its inhabitants. The aborigines of America may therefore be considered, at least for the purposes of history and archæology, as an autocthoneous people; and whatever civilization appeared before the discovery of Columbus, was indigenous civilization. The Mound Builders, therefore, were natives to the soil, and whatever advancement they made was their own invention, or was imparted to them by neighboring natives.

Indeed, while the Mound Builders may have resembled the Aztecs and the Peruvians in their form of government; yet in material advancement they differed much more widely from them and the extinct races of Central America, than from any of the Indian tribes that were found east of the Mississippi.

The Sioux and Cheyennes, the Comanches and Apaches, and other wandering tribes of the West, do not represent the mode of life of the Indians that lived east of the Mississippi. De Soto and his companions were struck with the novelty, when, in Arkansas or Missouri, they first encountered a tribe without fixed habitations, living in movable tents, and subsisting wholly by hunting and fishing. All the tribes east of the Mississippi were more or less agricultural. They all raised corn, beans, squashes, and melons. They pitched their camps and planted their villages on the borders of a stream. Many had permanent towns. When the French first landed at Montreal Island, they found Hocklehaga, an Indian town, fortified with a permanent palisade. The Iroquois had their villages, with corn-fields and orchards. The Cherokees and Creeks had fixed settlements of roomy, substantial houses. The Creeks had in each town an open public square, surrounded with their public buildings. The council-house of the Autose, or Snake tribe of the Creeks, was supported on columns carved to represent serpents, and the walls decorated with rude paintings. The town of the Uchees, the remnant of a tribe which the Creeks found in Georgia, when they arrived, and which they adopted into their confederacy, is described by Bartram, in 1773, as "the largest, most compact, and best situated Indian town I ever saw: the habitations are large and neatly built; the walls of the houses are constructed of a wooden frame, then lathed and plastered inside and out with a reddish, well-tempered clay, or mortar, which gives them the appearance of red brick walls, and these houses are neatly covered or footed with cypress bark, or the shingles of that tree."

Carver, exploring the Northwest, in 1766, described the town of the Sankies (Sacs) as "the largest and best built Indian town he ever saw. It contained about ninety houses, each large enough for several families, built up of hewn plank neatly jointed, and covered so compactly with bark as to keep out the most penetrating rains. Before the doors were placed comfortable sheds in which the inhabitants sat, when the weather would permit, and smoked their pipes. The streets were both regular and spacious, appearing more like a civilized town than the abode of savages."

Though it was not common, except in the South, to have their towns permanently fortified, it was common to intrench themselves, in time of war, with stockade defenses.

In some respects the Mound Builders and the modern Indians were alike. I have already said there is no recognized difference between the stone implements of the two. Both were great smokers, and lavished all their artistic skill in carving and beautifying their pipes. The Mound Builders appear to have kept their infants strapped to boards, as the Indians do. This inference was drawn by Morton and by Squire from the flatness of the occiput of the skull. The same characteristic is noted by Mr. Jones in an authentic skull recently disinterred in Georgia. They appear to have had similar amusements. The Natchez, Choctaws, Cherokees, and other Southern tribes, and also the Mandans, in the Northwest, were much addicted to a game called *chungke* by the Choctaws and Mandans, and *nettecawaw* by the Cherokees.

The game was played with disks of hard stone, that were greatly prized on account of the labor required to rub such hard stone into the required shape. These same stone disks, called by Squire and Davis discoid stones, were used by the Mound Builders. It is, however, only an inference that they were used for the same purpose.

And while one great difference between the Mound Builders and the modern Indians is that, among the former, the men must have labored; while among Indians labor is left to the squaws, still the difference was not absolute. For the Choctaws worked habitually in their corn-fields with the squaws, and even hired themselves out to the French as laborers.

WHAT BECAME OF THEM.

As to the final question, what became of the Mound Builders, little can be said beyond conjecture. Civilization, as a rule, radiates from a centre; and when, from

Some Considerations on the Mound Builders. 73

any cause, it fades out, it contracts upon the centre. Now, the vast stone temples and palaces of Central America are, at least, as old as the mounds of the United States. Central America was, then, relatively the birthplace and centre of aboriginal American civilization. The influence spread northward to the Mississippi and Ohio valleys.

So the Mound Builders appear to have receded from the lakes to the South. The Ohio Valley, when first discovered, was uninhabited. In the latter part of the seventeenth century, the entire region from Lake Erie to the Tennessee river was an unpeopled solitude. The ancient inhabitants may have died out from pestilence, or natural decay, or partly from some such custom as prevailed among the Natchez, of killing all the attendants of a chief upon his death. But it is more probable they were driven away.

The existing remains show they had, north of the Ohio river, a strong line of fortresses, along the Great Miami from its mouth to Piqua, with advanced works near Oxford and Eaton, and with a massive work in rear of this line, on the Little Miami, at Fort Ancient. There was another line crossing the Scioto Valley at Chillicothe, and extending west up the valley of Paint Creek. These seem to have constituted a line of permanent defense.

The situations were well chosen, were naturally very strong, and were fortified with great labor and some skill. Such works, if defended, could not have been taken by assault by any means the natives possessed, and they were so constructed as to contain a supply of water.

74   *Some Considerations on the Mound Builders.*

They would not be abandoned until the nations that held them were broken.

When these were abandoned, there was no retreat, except across the Ohio. South of the Ohio, in Kentucky and Tennessee, there are many works of defense, but none possessing the massive character of permanent works like the Ohio system. They are, comparatively, temporary works, thrown up for an exigency—are moreover isolated, not forming, as in Ohio, a connected system. They are such works as a people capable of putting up the Ohio forts might erect, while being gradually pushed south, and fighting an invader from the north or northwest.

South of the Tennessee river the indications are different. We miss there the forts that speak of prolonged and obstinate conflict. And we find among the tribes, as they were when first discovered, lingering traces of what we have called characteristic traits of the Mound Builders. The Indian tribes there, as a rule, had more substantial dwellings than those of the North; their towns were more permanent and better constructed; it was common in De Soto's time, and in some tribes even two hundred years later, for families to have separate farms; the chiefs were treated with a deference which was never seen among Northern Indians. Among the Natchez so late as 1730 the Great Sun was absolute despot; and in the accounts of De Soto's expedition, not only the romantic narrative of Garcilaso de la Vega, but in the more sober account of the Portuguese cavalier and the business like report of Biedma, we read of chiefs being carried in canopied litters by their subjects; and of the haughty chief Tuscalusa, sitting on a pile of cushions, with officers and attendants ranged about, and with a colored shield held aloft by one to screen him from the sun. Some tribes, the Natchez and Tensas, preserved till 1730 their temples with the holy perpetual fire. In De Soto's time chiefs commonly had their dwellings on the summit of the terraced mounds; and later several tribes used the rectangular inclosures, like the one that used to stand about where Eighth Street Park now is, in Cincinnati, as ground for playing the game *chungke*, with just such discoid stones as are found among the relics of the Mound Builders.

These remaining traces of the former population indicate that in the Southern States they were not absolutely exterminated, and swept off, leaving a void to be filled by a new unmingled race ; but that rather, in the interminable wars and restless emigrations of the more recent Indians, the less warlike Mound Builders gradually dwindled, and became absorbed in their conquerors. The Iroquois, pushing their conquering expeditions to Montreal and Mackinac, to North Carolina and the Mississippi, received and adopted many individuals from tribes they overcame, and remnants of tribes they had substantially exterminated. The Creeks, moving from their original home in the far West, came upon the Alibamas ; drove them in a pursuit, which lasted many years, to the Mississippi, across it, and finally into Alabama, when the chase ended, and the subdued remnant of the Alibamas was received into the Creek nation. The Natchez, after receiving remnants of several nearly extinct tribes, were so nearly exterminated by the French that the few remaining families fled to the Chickasaws and were absorbed. So the Mandans, the most

76 *Some Considerations on the Mound Builders.*

civilized tribe of the Northwest, dwindled away under the continued attacks of the Sioux, abandoned village after village, shifted their homes, till there is now but a feeble handful, living for safety with another tribe.

While the Mound Builders probably died out in the South thus gradually, and became absorbed in the tribes that overcame them, there is color for the suggestion often made, that the Natchez may have been a true remnant of that race. They stood apart from other tribes by their superiority in the simple arts practiced by Indians. They were so skillful making their red-stained pottery that Du Pratz had them make for him a set of plates for table use. But they were more distinguished from the others by their rites and government. They and the Tensas, an affiliated tribe, had temples where guardians perpetually preserved the holy fire. The Great Sun, their head chief, had absolute authority, and his person was sacred. They had an hereditary nobility. The words and phrases of address and salutation used toward the nobles, were wholly different from those used toward the common people.

The temple stood on a flat mound eight feet high, having a graded ascent. And at the annual corn feast a flat mound two feet high was erected, on which was built a house for the Sun, who was borne two miles to it in a litter carried by his subjects. After being carried around the gathered heap of corn, he alighted, saluted the grain, commanded his subjects to eat, and then it was lawful for them to touch it.

When they fled to Louisiana, in 1730, they surrounded themselves with a fort. Pickett, in his history of Alabama; Squire, in his Aboriginal Monu-

Some Considerations on the Mound Builders. 77

ments of New York, and other writers, say the Natchez also threw up mounds here. But neither Du Pratz, Charlevoix, Bossu, nor Dumont, make any such statement, and I have not access to any other cotemporary authority. Monette asserts that the works near Trinity were then constructed by the Natchez. But works of such magnitude could not have been constructed by the Natchez in the short time they were in this, their last fastness.

The Natchez claimed that in former days they had five hundred villages, and their borders stretched to the Ohio. But that wars and a devastating pestilence that broke out in old times, when a drowsy guardian suffered the holy fire to go out, had reduced them. To these causes Du Pratz added their custom of killing the attendants of a chief upon the chief's death. It is quite possible that the Natchez were a remnant of the race that constructed the mounds. If not, they must have been long in contact with that race.

Of the works on the upper Missouri, except the one described by Lewis and Clark, I have met no account, except the concise statement of Mr. Barrandt of his observations in 1869 and 1870. From the fact that he cut down a tree six hundred years old, growing on one of them, it is reasonable to suppose they were about cotemporaneous with the works in Ohio. A speculation, but a mere speculation, may be ventured as to the disappearance of their builders.

Lewis and Clark, and afterward Catlin, found on the upper Missouri three small neighboring tribes, who lived in towns of tolerably substantial and quite commodious mud houses, forming villages fortified with stockade and ditch. These little tribes resided in their secure villages, raising corn, and selling it to Western tribes for pelfries, which they sold in turn to the East, and venturing out only short distances to kill buffalo; while the whole region else was occupied by roving tribes, without any fixed habitation, and living wholly by the chase.

Of these three tribes—Rickarees, Mandans, and Minnetarees—the Rickarees are a fragment of the Pawnee nation ; the Minnetarees belong to the Dakota family; while the Mandans have no affiliation with any other known family. Morton, indeed, says they belong to the Dakota race, while De Smet says, on the other hand, they belong to the wholly different race, the great Chippeway family of tribes. Catlin, however, who lived some time among them, says their language has no affinity with any other he was acquainted with ; that, being a mere handful of a tribe, they learned to speak the language of other tribes, while none learned theirs.

The Mandans ever since they were first known, have enjoyed a reputation, as compared with their neighbors, somewhat like that of the Natchez in the South. They have been called "the polite and friendly Mandans," "the white Indians." Their huts, fifty feet in diameter, are described by Catlin as scrupulously neat ; the separate bedsteads were screened off by curtains of dressed skins ; a solid stockade and ditch defended their village, which was built on a precipitous bluff projecting into the river. They made a great variety of excellent pottery, which they baked in kilns ; and manufactured a sort of iridescent beads, which were highly prized for ornament. They played the game called "chungke" as it was played a hundred and fifty years ago in the South, and called it by the same name. Ever since they were first known, they have been wasting away under the relentless hostility of the Sioux, and are now almost wholly extinct, though the ruins of their former villages can be seen for many miles along the river.

It is stated by Catlin, as a fact, acknowledged by all three of these little tribes, that the Rickarees and Minnetarees merely adopted the habits of the Mandans after settling in their neighborhood. But no explanation has been given of the source whence the Mandans acquired their mode of life, so exceptional in that region.

Catlin suggests that they are descendants of the Mound Builders driven from Ohio. But there is nothing to warrant that; and they have no tradition of having come from any remote country. If we must make them descendants of Mound Builders, we need not go away from the valley of the upper Missouri for an ancestry. All that can be said, and that is mere speculation, is, it is possible that the Mandans are a lingering remnant of the ancient race that constructed the works on the upper Missouri, or of a tribe that by contact with that race imbibed some of its modes of life.

SOME WORKS IN TENNESSEE.

Before closing I desire to say a few words about some works near Savannah, Tenn., described in the Smithsonian octavo for 1871, by J. Parish Stelle. On the river bluff, about two miles below Savannah, is a group of mounds of the ordinary type; but at the foot of the bluff, in the swampy land between it and the river,

Some Considerations on the Mound Builders.

is a long intrenchment, not wholly obliterated. At regular intervals, the tracing of this intrenchment projects to the front, so as to make flank defenses, or rudimentary bastions, eighty yards apart. On the edge of the town, on the river bluff, is another group of mounds. This group of mounds is inclosed on the side away from the river by a double line of intrenchment, each like the one just described. One of the mounds, eight feet high, stands on a slope. In constructing it three trenches were first dug in the surface of the ground, and then arched over with tempered clay, making three furnaces. Rows of upright sticks or logs appear then to have been placed between these furnaces, partly for the purpose of protecting them from too great pressure. The mound was then made by throwing on earth. But flues of tempered clay were made, some extending directly up to the upper surface of the mound, others sinuously winding through it, so as to convey heat to every part. Logs of green wood were interspersed thickly through the mound and bits of dry wood placed about them. When the mound was opened all the wood was found reduced to charcoal, and the whole mound baked almost to brick. In another of the group were found fragments of burned clay flues and bits of charcoal. The first has the appearance of an elaborately constructed charcoal pit, from which the charcoal has not been removed; the other, one from which the charcoal had been taken. A tree, growing on one of the mounds, was found to be two hundred and fifteen years old. The other mounds were found to contain some bits of pottery and a few stone implements. While these last are undoubtedly works of the natives, it is not easy to believe that the in-

Some Considerations on the Mound Builders. 81

trenchments and charcoal mound were not made by Europeans.

De Soto, marching north across Alabama, reached a river which he crossed in boats that he built, in December, 1540. He took possession of the little Indian town Chicaca, and went into winter-quarters. The Indians made a sudden night attack, set fire to the town, and the surprised Spaniards lost everything. De Soto gathered all the fragments of metal from the ashes, moved to another town half a league off, and there tempered the sword blades and made new lances, saddles, and implements. Herrera says, De Soto fortified this camp of refuge.

This Chicaca has been generally supposed to have been in the northern part of the present State of Mississippi. But it may be that the works two miles below Savannah mark its site, while the group on the edge of the town of Savannah, including the charcoal mound, may indicate the place where De Soto repaired his armament.

NOTES.

A. "*Native silver . . . . . hammered into leaf, and wrapped around small copper ornaments.* p. 67. The silver-coated copper bosses, found by Dr. Hildreth at the bottom of one of the Marietta mounds, and now in the college museum at Marietta, have occasioned much perplexity. Squire says, in the appendix to his "Aboriginal Monuments of New York :" " These articles have been critically examined, and it is beyond doubt that the copper bosses are absolutely *plated*, not simply overlaid, *with silver*. Between the copper and the silver exists a connection, such as, it seems to me, could only be produced by heat; and if it is admitted that these are genuine remains of the mound-builders, it must at the same time be admitted that they possessed the difficult art of plating one metal on another."

This inference may not be necessary. It may be that the two metals were found naturally joined, and the compound fragments were simply hammered into shape. Mr. Cyrus Mendenhall, who spent many years on the shores of Lake Superior, tells me that bits of native silver are sometimes found joined with the copper as if welded to it; and that the miners sometimes hammer out from such fragments rings that have all the appearance of copper rings plated with silver.

B. *Withdrawal of the Natchez to Louisiana.* p. 77. Notwithstanding the amount of speculation upon the flight of the Natchez to Louisiana, the locality of their retreat has not been fixed and determined. And yet it seems susceptible of identification. Du Pratz says the French " went up the Red River, then

Notes.

the Black River, and from thence up the *Bayouc d'Argent*, which communicates with a small lake at no great distance from the fort which the Natchez had built."

Now, Mr. Dunbar, in his account of an exploration of Black River and its confluents, communicated by President Jefferson to Congress, along with the report of Lewis and Clark's expedition, says the Tensas, one of the confluents of the Black, " communicates with the Mississippi lowlands by the intervention of other creeks and lakes, and by one in particular, called *Bayou d'Argent*, which empties into the Mississippi about fourteen miles above Natchez. . . . . A large lake, called St. John's Lake, occupies a considerable part of the passage between the Mississippi and the Tensas, and has at some former period been the bed of the Mississippi."

This bayou and lake can be seen on the maps of Louisiana, between the parishes of Concordia and Tensas, and agree with the locality inscribed " Natchez destroyed " on Du Pratz's map.

The fort constructed here by the Natchez was undoubtedly a palisade. Charlevoix simply says they fortified themselves. Du Pratz says they built a fort. Dumont says, " they built a fort upon the model of the one from which they had been driven"— and that was a palisade. Dumont further says, " the troops pillaged the fort and set fire to it."

The Natchez were not actually exterminated. A band of them, escaping, crossed the country to the Red River and attacked the French fort at Natchitoches. Charlevoix says that here " they intrenched themselves." Dumont says they threw up an intrenchment—"*creuserent dans la plaine une espèce de retranchement où ils se fortifierent*." So far for contemporary authority. But Mr. John Sibley, in a letter concerning the Southern Indians, dated Natchitoches, April 5, 1805, and which letter was annexed to Jefferson's message already mentioned, says : "After the massacre of the French inhabitants of Natchez, by the Natchez Indians,

Notes. 85

in 1728, these Indians fled from the French, after being reinforced, and came up Red River, and camped about six miles below the town of Natchitoches, near the river, by the side of a small lake of clear water, and erected a mound of considerable size, where it now remains "

This statement is, I believe, the source of all the statements in the books that the Natchez, on their flight into Louisiana, built mounds.

C. *The Mandan Language.* p. 78. Lewis and Clark spent a winter with the Mandans, and Capt. Lewis' official report to the president says they speak " a primitive language, with some words resembling the Osages'." Prince Maximilian, of Wied, who spent some months among the Mandans, in 1833, says they speak a distinct language, differing radically from the Rickarees and Minnetarees.

ERRATA.

Page 17, last line, for " guessers," read " guesses."
Page 26, line 21, for " a Hindoo," read " the smallest Hindoo."
Page 40, line 6, for " periods," read " period."
Page 42, line 11, for " Pierce," read " Peirce."
Page 46, line 22, for " man is," read " is man."
Page 46, line 29, for " he," read " the."
Page 54, line 26, for " Barrand," read " Barrandt."
Page 63, line 3, after the word " years," insert the word " old."
Page 64, last line, after the word " Norwood," insert " Reading."
Page 65, line 21, for " country," read " county."
Page 70, line 3, for " autocthoneous," read " autochthonous."
Page 71, line 17, for " Sankies," read " Saukies."

JUL 26 1974 7 DAY USE
RETURN TO

ANTHROPOLOGY LIBRARY

This publication is due on the LAST DATE
and HOUR stamped below.

RB17—40m-8,'72
(Q4186S10)4188—A-32

General Library
University of California
Berkeley

Check Out More Titles From HardPress Classics Series In this collection we are offering thousands of classic and hard to find books. This series spans a vast array of subjects — so you are bound to find something of interest to enjoy reading and learning about.

Subjects:
Architecture
Art
Biography & Autobiography
Body, Mind &Spirit
Children & Young Adult
Dramas
Education
Fiction
History
Language Arts & Disciplines
Law
Literary Collections
Music
Poetry
Psychology
Science
…and many more.

Visit us at www.hardpress.net

"Beautiful gift.. lovely finish.
My Niece loves it, so precious!"

Helen R Brumfieldon

★★★★★

UNIQUE GIFT

FOR KIDS, PARTNERS AND FRIENDS

Timeless books such as:

Alice in Wonderland • The Jungle Book • The Wonderful Wizard of Oz
Peter and Wendy • Robin Hood • The Prince and The Pauper
The Railway Children • Treasure Island • A Christmas Carol

Romeo and Juliet • Dracula

Visit
ImTheStory.com
and order yours today!